2. Waltz

T0057062

Tempo di valse poco vivo (♩ =c.112)

3. Homage To J.S.B.

To Georgina Dobrée

FIVE PIECES FOR CLARINET
(unaccompanied)

GORDON JACOB

1. Preamble

Lento (♩ = c.46)

© 1973 Oxford University Press

Printed in Great Britain
OXFORD UNIVERSITY PRESS, MUSIC DEPARTMENT, GREAT CLARENDON STREET, OXFORD OX2 6DP
Photocopying this copyright material is ILLEGAL.

Gordon Jacob

FIVE
PIECES

for solo clarinet

Oxford University Press

4. Soliloquy

5. Scherzo and Trio

Allegro vivo (♩=c.132)

TRIO

Meno mosso

Allegro vivo

D.S. al FINE

Reproduced and printed by
Halstan & Co. Ltd., Amersham, Bucks., England

Engraved by PWM

ISBN 978-0-19-35736

9 780193 57368